Mood Boost

Contents

Written by Catherine Baker

Collins

If you groan when you think of doing sport, this book is for you!

trips out

gardening

Sport is good for you, but there are lots of things that help boost fitness and mood.

jobs

singing

Get out!

Scoot to the park, or travel on foot.

Plan a mood-boosting trip to the woods. Look for flowers, or spot frogs and snails.

Gardening

Grab a trowel and weed the flower beds! Digging is good for the arms and legs.

You can get good food from the soil, too.

So sweet! This boosts my mood!

Jobs

Help the adults and get fit too!

Sweep the stairs with a broom, or polish the car.

Singing

Singing is good for the lungs – and the brain!

Rocking out to a good song boosts my mood.

Keeping track of the steps keeps me fit and my brain fit, too.

Sport-free fitness

The tips in this book can help you keep fit. Lots of them are free, too.

But sport is good as well. Keep looking – perhaps there is a sport for you!

Keeping fit

Review: After reading

Use your assessment from hearing the children read to choose any GPCs, words or tricky words that need additional practice.

Read 1: Decoding

- On page 5, point to the phrase **mood-boosting**. Ask: Can you think of another phrase that means the same? (e.g. *uplifting, happy-making, cheering up*) To clarify, ask the children if they have suddenly felt happier than before. Ask: What boosted your mood?

- Focus on words with adjacent consonants. Check the children sound out all the consonants as they read these words:

  sport   brain   sweep   trowel   strength   scrambling   clearing

- Model reading the main text on page 7, slowly but fluently. Ask the children to read the speech bubble in the same way. Say: Can you blend the words in your head as you read them?

Read 2: Prosody

- Model reading page 12, using emphasis to sound enthusiastic and persuasive.

- Talk about how emphasising **you** and **free** gets the listener's attention.

- Discuss words to emphasise on page 13, then let the children read the page as persuasively as they can.

Read 3: Comprehension

- Discuss why the author might have chosen to write this book. Does she want to help people? How? (e.g. *she wants people to get fit; she suggests how people can keep fit; she gives activity ideas for people who don't like sport*)

- Challenge the children to skim or scan the text to answer these questions:

  o Are most of the activities the author suggests outdoor activities? (e.g. *yes, only two – clearing your room and cleaning are indoor only while all the others are, or could be done, outdoors*)

  o What can help you keep your brain fit? (*singing and keeping track of steps – pages 10 and 11*)

  o How can a tree make you fitter? (e.g. *you can scramble up it – page 4*)

- Look at pages 14 and 15 together and encourage the children to talk about the pictures. Ask them which of the activities they like to do and why. Or do they prefer another activity?